My Body is Special
and Belongs to Me!

Sally Berenzweig, MEd, MA
& Cherie Benjoseph, LCSW

Illustrated by Lilah Cohen

KidSafe ®
FOUNDATION
working together to keep kids safe

The information provided in this book is designed to provide helpful information on the subjects discussed. This book is not intended to replace the advice of or treatment by psychologists or other health care professionals.

FOUNDATION

KidSafe Foundation, Inc.
info@KidSafeFoundation.org
www.KidSafeFoundation.org

ISBN: 978-0-9989529-0-1

Printed in the United States
by Minuteman Press of Boca Raton, Florida.

Fourth printing

Thank you to all the adults who understand the importance of teaching personal safety education, support our programs, and read our books to their children.

Thank you to all the children who have enjoyed our books and have learned important safety skills. May you all stay KidSafe!

Working together to keep KidSafe,

Cherie and Sally

Cofounders of KidSafe Foundation

Foreword

Erin Merryn, survivor of child sexual abuse, on a mission to bring mandated education to children across the United States, shares why this book is essential to all parents.

Growing up in school each year I was educated with my classmates on tornado drills, fire drills, bus drills, stranger danger, and learned the eight ways to say "NO" to drugs. As a child I never had to take cover because of a real tornado. I never had to stop, drop, and roll or run out of a burning building. I never had to evacuate a school bus due to an emergency, but I had the knowledge to know what to do if any of those situations happened. Where was the drill on how to escape a child molester? Where was the lesson plan on sexual abuse, safe touches, and safe secrets? It never came. I was not educated on "How to Tell Today" or "How to Get Away." I was never educated on "My Body Belongs to Me." I was sexually abused starting at age 6. I was confused and scared. That my body seemed to belong to the men who used and abused it was the message I learned—because I was getting no other message.

> "Our children need to know they are not to blame and don't deserve to be hurt— helping them find their voice is crucial."

I was displaying all the signs of an abused child, yet nobody ever asked the simple questions, "Has someone hurt you?" "Do you have secrets with anyone?" "Does anyone make you feel uncomfortable?" There were many safe adults in my life, but they failed to give me the message, ***My body is special and belongs to me. I am in charge of my body as you can see.*** Had this book existed when I was a child—and been read to me—it would have empowered me to tell my story and could have saved me years of sexual abuse. These 19 pages could have saved my childhood and given me a voice. Imagine for a moment if this book were in the hands of my parents, teachers, social workers, and psychologists reading it to the once six-year old that I was in 1991. The answer they were all looking for would come out of the darkness. Because I was not taught how to keep my body safe, I ended up not showing myself love and care. I was one child that could not be saved, but millions more can if this book gets into the right hands. Save a child—let them know their body belongs to them.

> Merryn says, "safe touch, unsafe touch" and "how to get away and tell today"—are mantras she wants ingrained in today's kids.

Erin Merryn is author of *Stolen Innocence* and *Living for Today,* both memoirs about incest and rape. She has appeared on *Oprah, Good Morning America, CNN, Jane Velez Mitchell,* and *Montel.* Erin has also appeared in *Time Magazine, Cosmo Girl!, Chicago Tribune, Daily Herald,* and numerous others. She is the force behind Erin's law in Illinois, providing education on sexual abuse prevention for pre-K through 5th grade.

Introduction to KidSafe

With the purchase of this book, you are helping support the nonprofit organization **KidSafe Foundation**. Our mission is to educate children and adults in the prevention of child sexual abuse, bullying, and Internet dangers. Every child deserves the right to be safe, the right to use their Safety Voice, and the right to access help.

For more information about our programs, visit **www.kidsafefoundation.org**.

Why We Wrote This Book

Parents often ask us how they can talk to their children about Touch without scaring them—or even how to approach the topic, as they are often uncomfortable with the subject. In this day and age, we **must** talk to our children about the topic of Touch. When you talk to your child about Touches and their bodies, you are empowering them with safety skills. Knowledge is power. Offenders look for children without Prevention Education, those whose parents do not discuss these issues with them. With this book, it is our goal to make all children KidSafe smart.

As you read through this book with your child, you will discover ways you can talk with and teach your child about Safe and Unsafe Touch in a non-frightening and developmentally appropriate manner. This book is the conversation you want to have—but perhaps are not sure how to approach. *My Body Is Special and Belongs to ME!* provides you with a framework for many on-going conversations with your children about all types of Touch.

We ask that you take a few minutes to read through to the end of the book before you share the story with your child. You will find the Parent's Place in the back of the book. There we discuss with you the most common questions and concerns parents have, the myth of stranger danger, and a section on Conversation Starters—questions to ask your children—with answers to enhance communication and tips on how to integrate the language of safety into your daily parenting. For further information, please visit our website at www.kidsafefoundation.org for resources and links to access help if needed. Wishing you many great reads!

Working together to keep KidSafe,

Cherie and Sally

I am KidSafe smart and I have a lot to share
about keeping our bodies safe
and treating ourselves with
love and care.

Because My Body Is Special and belongs to me.
I am in charge of my body, as you will see!

I will share many things about what to do
to help keep your body safe and take
    good care of you.
As you read this book, you will see
kids who listen to their Safety Voice,
    like me!

When you listen to your Safety Voice
    and think about how a touch feels inside,
You can use those feelings as your
    Safe and Unsafe touch guide.

So think about how many times we are touched throughout the day,
We know a touch is Safe when we feel this way:
Happy, cozy, and comfortable as can be.
A touch that feels this way is a Safe touch to me.

4

When my friend holds my hand, it is a Safe touch to me.
Because I feel warm, comfy, and as joyful as can be.

I love when my Mom or Dad tucks me in at night.
A kiss on my forehead and I feel everything is alright.

When my teacher pats me on the back
and says, "You are so smart,"
I feel proud and special
with a cozy feeling in my heart.

But sometimes a touch
can make you feel bad.
Being pushed on the
playground
might make you feel mad.

8

If my hair was pulled,
  it would really hurt me.
I would feel sad and uncomfortable;
  an unsafe touch it would be.

My sister likes to tickle me,
    and it can feel real good.
I feel special and loved;
just like a brother and sister
    should.

That was too much, Sis.

When I want her to stop
    because it no longer feels good,
I use my Safety Voice to stop her
    and I hope that she would.

Taking care of my body is
   something I am learning to do.
Washing and dressing are now
   my jobs, too.

You can learn to take care of your body, just like me.
Our bodies are special, as you can see.

I have private parts that belong just to me.
They are under my bathing suit,
   but I won't let you see.

You have private parts
   that are special, too.
No one should touch them—
they are meant just for YOU!

But if I have a rash or my private parts
   don't feel like they should,
my parents take me to the Doctor and
   if she needs to see them, she could.

Because My Body Is Special and belongs to me.
I am in charge of my body, as you can see!

If you get a touch on your private parts,
  and you feel weird and confused in your heart,
Try to use your Safety Voice as fast as you can.
Go tell a grown-up—they will understand.

Great job Reporting! I am so glad you came to tell me.

It is never your fault if you get
  a touch that is confusing to you.
Make sure you tell a grown-up,
  because they will know what to do.

Your Circle of Safe Adults is where you should go.
When you have a problem, these adults need to know.

Don't keep it inside, share what is bothering you.
So you can get the help you need and stay safe, too!

Most touches make us feel
comfortable, special,
    and safe.
Getting a hug from
    someone you love
can make you feel
    great.

So now say these words with me.
Believe it, and it will come to be:

MY BODY IS SPECIAL AND BELONGS TO ME.
I AM IN CHARGE OF MY BODY, AS YOU CAN SEE!

18

So as we end this book
  I will go give a hug
to someone who is special,
  to someone I love.

19 You can give someone you love a hug, too.
It's always your choice, because your body belongs to YOU!

Your Circle of Safe Adults is where you should go.
Who are YOUR safe adults? Use this circle to show.

My Circle of Safe Adults

PARENT'S PLACE

Welcome to the wonderful world of talking with your children about Touch. This book provides you with a framework for many ongoing conversations about Safe and Unsafe Touch. Teaching your children about Touch is an important aspect of everyday parenting.

Now that you are open to the topic of Touch, it is time to empower yourself and your child. By sharing this book with children, you are teaching them that their bodies are special and belong to them. Here are some questions parents often ask regarding talking with their children about Touch.

When and why should I start teaching my children the proper names for their private parts? What are the proper names for private parts?

As early as age three, children can learn the proper names for their body parts, including their private parts. In this book we use the term *private parts* for the parts of the body covered by a bathing suit. Teaching children the correct names for their body parts is the first step in empowering them to understand that their body is special and belongs to them. Some proper names to teach your child for private parts are *vulva, vagina, penis, testicles, breasts,* and *buttocks.* As we say in our adult seminars, "An elbow is an elbow, and a penis is a penis."

It is as simple as that. If you find it uncomfortable, get in front of the mirror and say, "Penis. Vagina." a hundred times or until you lose your discomfort. Why? Because you need to be comfortable talking about private parts so your children will feel comfortable talking about them with you. By simply giving them the vocabulary to be able to talk openly about their bodies, you are giving them a powerful tool to counter exploitation and abuse. The next section presents more information on this topic.

Are you comfortable talking about sexuality? Private parts? Touch?

Often, parents and caregivers express their own discomfort about talking directly with their children about private parts and Safe and Unsafe Touch. Your child will easily pick up on your negative, nonverbal body language

> *By sharing this book with children, you are teaching them that their bodies are special and belong to them.*

> *By simply giving them the vocabulary to be able to talk openly about their bodies, you are giving them a powerful tool to counter exploitation and abuse.*

> *". . . a great tool for parents to bridge the gap in discussing sensitive issues with their children."*
> —Annmarie Watler, Commander, Investigative Section, North Miami Police Department

21

and think, *Oh, this is something we can't or don't talk about,* thereby cutting off communication. When you show discomfort talking about Touch or your body, you send a subliminal message to your child that discussing these topics is taboo. This will shut down a child's appropriate natural inquisitiveness, often sending him or her elsewhere to get information.

Your children need to know that you are an approachable parent and that they can come to you to discuss their bodies without fear or discomfort. Take the time to process where your discomfort stems from. By utilizing resources such as this book, you will empower yourself with the knowledge to become your child's best teacher.

What do I do when my child won't give a kiss or hug to my relatives?

Often, we are asked by a parent if they should force their child to hug or kiss a relative when they don't want to. We always tell them, "Don't do it!" When you compel a child to touch an adult whom they don't want to, you are telling the child that the wants and needs of the adult are more important than the child's own wants and needs.

We suggest you talk to your child in advance, using an alternate plan of action that may include substituting a "high-five" or responding with a polite *No thank you.* Through this discussion, you are sending the message to your child that you respect their body and their wishes and letting them know that they are allowed to make their own choices with regard to touching and being touched. Also, be sure to tell other caregivers in your child's life that you are teaching your child personal safety life-skills—and share this important lesson on Touch with them, too.

How can you help your child to distinguish a Safe Touch from an Unsafe Touch?

The goal of this book is to teach children that they can judge a touch as Safe or Unsafe by how the touch makes them feel and by knowing the personal boundaries of their private parts. This association between physical touch and feelings is an important part in the process of children understanding when the line of safe or appropriate touch has been

---

When you show discomfort talking about Touch or your body, you are sending a subliminal message to your child that discussing these topics is taboo.

When you compel a child to touch an adult whom they don't want to, you are telling that child that the wants and needs of the adult are more important than the child's own wants and needs.

The goal of this book is to teach children that they can judge a touch as Safe or Unsafe by how the touch makes them feel . . .

22

crossed. In conversations with your child, emphasize that no one should be touching or looking at their private parts and that they shouldn't be touching or looking at anyone else's private parts.

Explain that an Unsafe Touch on a private part might make them feel *confused,* weird, embarrassed, awkward, hurt, betrayed, or sad, even though sometimes it might also feel "good." This is why it's confusing for children to decide. Stress the boundaries: your body is special and nobody touches your private parts. If they ever get touched there, they need to report it to a trusted adult immediately. It is **not** okay for **any** adult to touch them on their private parts—even if the adult who gave them the touch is someone special to them. Stress that *your body is special and belongs to you;* so no matter who it is, the child should seek help to stop the touching. They **must** report it because even if it "feels good," it is **not** a safe touch.

Using this dialogue in an ongoing, age-appropriate manner will help your child make safer and smarter choices about their bodies as they grow into pre-teens and teens.

Talking About Touch in Everyday Life

The terms *Safe Touch, Unsafe Touch, Private Parts,* and *Reporting* should and can easily become part of your family's everyday vocabulary. We call these words *KidSafe Key Concepts.*

Example: You are at home and your child falls and gets hurt. Another child —a sibling or friend—approaches, gently touches the child, and asks if they are okay. You can say to the child who is being touched, "How did it feel when Jan touched you on the shoulder?" Help them put words to it: *nice, happy, comfortable.* Ask, "Was that a Safe Touch or an Unsafe Touch for you?" *Safe touch.* Commend the other child for their positive response.

Example: Children are in the classroom or playroom. While arguing over a toy they are playing with, one child reaches out and hits the other. Ask the hitter, "Was that a Safe or Unsafe Touch? How else could you have handled this situation?" Be prepared with appropriate consequences for the hitter to send the message that problems aren't solved with unsafe touches.

. . . an Unsafe Touch on a private part might make them feel confused, weird, embarrassed, or sad, even though sometimes it might also feel "good."

Using this dialogue in an ongoing, age-appropriate manner will help your child make safer and smarter choices about their bodies as they grow into pre-teens and teens.

KidSafe Key Concepts: The terms Safe Touch, Unsafe Touch, Private Parts, and Reporting should and can easily become part of your family's everyday vocabulary.

What is a *Safety Voice*?

The term *Safety Voice* is used to teach children about the "little voice" inside their heads that can help them stop and think in order to make safer and smarter choices. Once they realize that something is not safe, children can use their safety voice—aloud—to report to a trusted adult. We use this term in regard to the child distinguishing a safe touch from an unsafe touch, and then talking about it using his or her actual voice.

What is the difference between *Tattling* and *Reporting*?

As we teach children personal safety, we always need to have a discussion about the difference between *tattling* and *reporting.*

Children often get confused between the concept of *tattling*—telling on someone just to get them in trouble—and *reporting.* They should always report when it relates to the safety of themselves and others; seeking help from an adult when they or someone else is at risk of getting hurt or has already gotten hurt. We ask children regularly throughout the lessons, "Is that tattling or reporting?" You can ask the same question when your child approaches you at home with a situation.

When you teach your child personal safety life-skills you (and we) break the cycle of silence that surrounds child abuse. Children are often scared into silence. However, a child who is taught that he or she has rights—and has learned how to report to a trusted grown-up when faced with a safety situation—becomes the first line of defense in his or her own safety.

Why do we no longer teach children about *Stranger Danger*?

In today's world we do not teach *Stranger Danger,* a concept we learned as children. Why? Statistically, 90% of the time a child is sexually, physically, or emotionally abused it is by someone they know and often love and trust. 68% of the time the abuse comes from a close family member.

The statistics of abuse are staggering: 1 in 3 girls and 1 in 6 boys will be sexually exploited by the age of 18. Most cases of abuse still go unreported, so these statistics do not tell the full story. Since the majority of abuse is perpetrated by a trusted and often loved adult, it makes reporting abuse even more difficult for a child.

Who are the people that hurt children?

Immediate family members such as fathers, stepfathers, brothers, mothers, stepmothers; and extended family such as cousins, aunts and uncles, grandparents; and close family friends. Most child molesters take on jobs or volunteer work involving children, such as coaches, teachers, clergy (all religions), camp counselors and swim instructors, babysitters, music instructors and other tutors (especially one-on-one), Boy Scout leaders, child care workers . . . anybody.

It is important to understand that most offenders are heterosexual men and male teenagers (half of all offenders start offending by age 14), well educated, middle class, upstanding citizens (many with children of their own) who know their victims. However, these offenders can come in every shape, size, ethnicity, and socioeconomic group—and can even be female.

Why wouldn't my child tell me about abuse?

Sexual offenders are smart and savvy and take you and your child through a process called *grooming*. Grooming is the means by which offenders gain your trust and the trust of your child. This is why both parents and children need to be aware of the signs of grooming and keep the lines of communication open. The grooming process often happens slowly—it could take a day, a week, a month, or even more than a year. These offenders take their time to make sure they have obtained the trust of the child.

Grooming progresses in the following stages:

Stage 1: Friendship & Trust—Offender begins the process of befriending the child (oftentimes the family as well).

Stage 2: Gifts & Rewards—Offender may give your child gifts or do special favors for him or her.

Stage 3: Secrets & Threats—Offender asks a child to keep a secret to see if they will.

Stage 4: Abuse Begins—Offender begins abuse, believing he or she has a willing participant.

The statistics of abuse are staggering: 1 in 3 girls and 1 in 6 boys will be sexually exploited by the age of 18.

"I often tell parents to beware of any adult who wants to be with your children more than you do . . . beware of anyone who seems too good to be true."
—KEN LANNING

(Expert on the issue of victimization of children, former F.B.I. Special Agent–Behavioral Science Unit and National Center for the Analysis of Violent Crime, founding member of the Board of Directors of the American Professional Society on the Abuse of Children)

Grooming is the process by which offenders gain your trust and the trust of your child.

What are some warning signs that you and your child are being groomed?

- Adult taking undue interest in a child
- Adult spending time alone with a child or children
- Adult offering to babysit
- Adult giving gifts or money to a child
- Adult using inappropriate language such as "you are my best friend"
- Adult allowing the child to get away with inappropriate behavior
- Adult trying to tickle, wrestle, hold, hug, or kiss a child, thereby desensitizing the child to their touch

Our children have the right to be safe and enjoy their childhood. As parents, we have the obligation to be aware of the safety issues affecting our children—and teach them the skills they need to be safe.

CONTINUE THE LEARNING

Parents, continue the learning at home with *Jack Teaches His Friends to Be KidSafe!,* the first book in the KidSafe SAFE AND SMART SERIES. This book for children ages 3 through 10 teaches essential personal safety skills for children—skills for a lifetime—and encourages the use of a language of safety for your home.

We hope that you share this book with other parents and keep the conversation going. The more you and your children talk openly about these issues, the safer they will be.

For more information about KidSafe—and for helpful resources— visit our website at www.kidsafefoundation.org

CONVERSATION STARTERS

Questions to Ask Your Children

Q: *What is a Safe Touch?*
A: A Safe Touch is a touch that makes you feel safe, comfortable, warm, loved, cozy, happy, and relaxed. For example: holding hands, pat on back, hug or kiss from someone you love.

Q: *What is an Unsafe Touch?*
A: An Unsafe Touch is a touch that makes you feel sad, mad, *confused,* unsafe, uncomfortable, nervous, scared, embarrassed, awkward, hurt, betrayed, weird. For example: hitting, kicking, biting, pulling hair, excessive tickling, or touching private parts.

Q: *What should you do if you get a touch you feel confused about?* Or: *What should you do if you get a touch you are not sure is a Safe or Unsafe Touch?*
A: Report to a grown-up you trust as soon as you can, and keep reporting (telling) until somebody listens.

Q: *Where are your private parts?*
A: All the parts covered by your bathing suit.

Q: *What are a boy's private parts? What are a girl's private parts?*
A: Boy: penis, testicles. Girl: vulva, vagina, breasts. Both: buttocks.

Q: *When is it okay for an adult to touch or look at your private parts?*
A: **Infants to Age 4:** During washing, bathing, or personal hygiene in the bathroom; when a child approaches their grown-up with a rash, injury, or illness which needs care; when a doctor needs to examine your private parts and your grown-up is with you. At this very young age, an abuser—family member, babysitter, nanny, daycare provider—often begins to desensitize a child to Unsafe Touch under the guise of helping with hygiene, playing a

> A **Safe Touch** is a touch that makes you feel safe, comfortable, warm, loved, cozy, happy, and relaxed.
>
> An **Unsafe Touch** is a touch that makes you feel sad, mad, confused, unsafe, uncomfortable, nervous, scared, embarrassed, awkward, hurt, betrayed, weird.

"special" game, etc. It is of dire importance for adults to be aware of who is caring for their child, as well as any changes in their child's mood and behavior around certain people, along with any physical issues. To this end, we support the use of "nanny cams" in the home.

This is what makes knowing how to use proper names for body parts so important: if a child needs to report an unsafe touch thay can make it clear what has happened. Refer to the section on grooming for more specifics.

A: **Ages 4 to 8:** Generally, we encourage children of this age group to become independent, but supervised, in their personal hygiene. Touching or looking at private parts at this age is appropriate when a child approaches his or her grown-up with a rash, injury, or illness which needs care; or when a doctor needs to examine their private parts and a grown-up is present.

Q: *Is it okay to say no to ANY adult who wants to hug or kiss you?*
A: Yes. Your body belongs to you and you are in charge of whether you want to give or receive a touch. Instead, you can shake hands, give a high-five, or say *No thank you.*

Q: *Who would you go to for help if you got an Unsafe Touch?*
A: This is an activity you can do with your child (see the Circle of Safe Adults activity on page 20). Have your child draw three adults they trust and label them. Then discuss with your child who they chose and why. Make sure you are comfortable with whom they would go to for help and be certain to tell the chosen adults they are part of your child's Circle of Safe Adults.

Q: *What was a Safe Touch you had today?*
A: EXAMPLES: My friend helped me up when I fell down. I hugged mommy when I got off the bus. My dad kissed me goodnight, etc.

Q: *What was an Unsafe Touch you had today?*
A: EXAMPLES: I got pushed at the playground. I got kicked in the shin at soccer practice (accidentally). My piano teacher put his hand on my leg and I was uncomfortable.

Have your child draw three adults they trust and label them. Then discuss with your child who they chose and why. Make sure you are comfortable with whom they would go to for help and be certain to tell the chosen adults they are part of your child's **Circle of Safe Adults.**

About the Authors

Sally Berenzweig, MEd, MA, Child Safety Expert, Mental Health Professional, Educator, Public Speaker, Author, Mom, and Cofounder of KidSafe Foundation

Sally Berenzweig is a former psychotherapist who has a Masters in Elementary Education and a Masters in Counseling Psychology. She has worked with survivors of sexual abuse as well as in private practice. She specializes in child safety, prevention education workshops, and parenting skills. Sally is the co-author of *KidSafe for Kids,* an 8-week curriculum for children ages 4–11, and two children's books *Jack Teaches His Friends to Be KidSafe!* and the 2011 Literary Award Winning children's book *My Body Is Special and Belongs to ME!*

KidSafe co-founders Sally Berenzweig (top) and Cherie Benjoseph.

Cherie Benjoseph, LCSW, Child Safety Expert, Mental Health Professional, Educator, Public Speaker, Author, Mom, and Cofounder of KidSafe Foundation

Cherie has been working in the field of social work since 1989, specializing in children and families. After earning her MSW from Boston University, Cherie took a position as a public school guidance counselor (School Social Worker) in Boston. There she had the opportunity to work with early intervention through middle school students, teachers, and parents. She trained and specialized in violence prevention/conflict resolution, active parenting skills, and her main focus, personal safety. Cherie is the coauthor of *KidSafe for Kids,* an 8-week curriculum for children ages 4–11, and two children's books *Jack Teaches His Friends to Be KidSafe!* and the 2011 Literary Award Winning children's book *My Body Is Special and Belongs to ME!*

For more information about the authors or KidSafe Foundation's programs, please visit www.kidsafefoundation.org

About the Illustrator

Lilah Cohen is a seventeen-year-old honors student who resides in Florida. She lives with her parents, both of whom are employed in law enforcement, three younger siblings and her cat, Red. Her two sisters and brother often serve as inspiration for her drawings. Lilah has been drawing for as long as she can remember and has taken various art courses since she was five. When she is not drawing, Lilah enjoys reading and is an avid fan of art and history.

About the Designer

Gary A. Rosenberg is a graphic designer specializing in books targeted to specific audiences. He met Sally's son, Jack, teaching self defense to local kids, and the collaboration here is an extension of that relationship. He is also co-author (with wife, Carol) of the Jon and Jayne Doe Series of books on socialization for teens and pre-teens (www.jonandjayne.com). Gary works with Carol from their studio in Boca Raton, Florida, serving the editorial and graphic needs of the book publishing industry. For more info, visit www.thebookcouple.com.